Written by Eileen Raycroft and developed by
Alchemy II, Inc.
Illustrated by Pat Paris Productions

Published by Checkerboard Press, a division of Macmillan, Inc.
CHECKERBOARD PRESS and colophon are trademarks of Macmillan, Inc.

Designed by Pat Paris

10 9 8 7 6 5 4 3 2 1

ISBN 0-02-688821-1

An opening note . . .

You probably already know or are even responsible for a lot of things in this world that are just *not* hot. Like, have you ever worn your athletic socks (the white ones with the colorful stripes around the top) with a pair of dress pants? Take it easy, even all the formerly un-cool dudes in this world needed a little help in the beginning.

After minutes, no, make that *hours* of intense, painstaking research (in the jacuzzi), here it is—a beautifully illustrated example of "What's Hot and What's Not." Guiding you along the path of social acceptance and peer approval, we remain yours truly,

Being health-conscious and drinking bottled water is hot.

Developing a hernia hauling all those bottles of water in from the car is not.

Buying a cool 4-wheel drive truck is hot.

Forgetting about the size of the garage doorway is not.

Racquetball is *definitely* hot . . .

. . . Just be sure not to take your eyes off the ball.

Taking your trail horse out for a ride on your ranch is hot.

. . . But don't forget to tighten the saddle.

It's hot to work out first thing in the morning before work . . .

. . . just don't overdo it!

Wearing the latest expensive sneakers is hot.

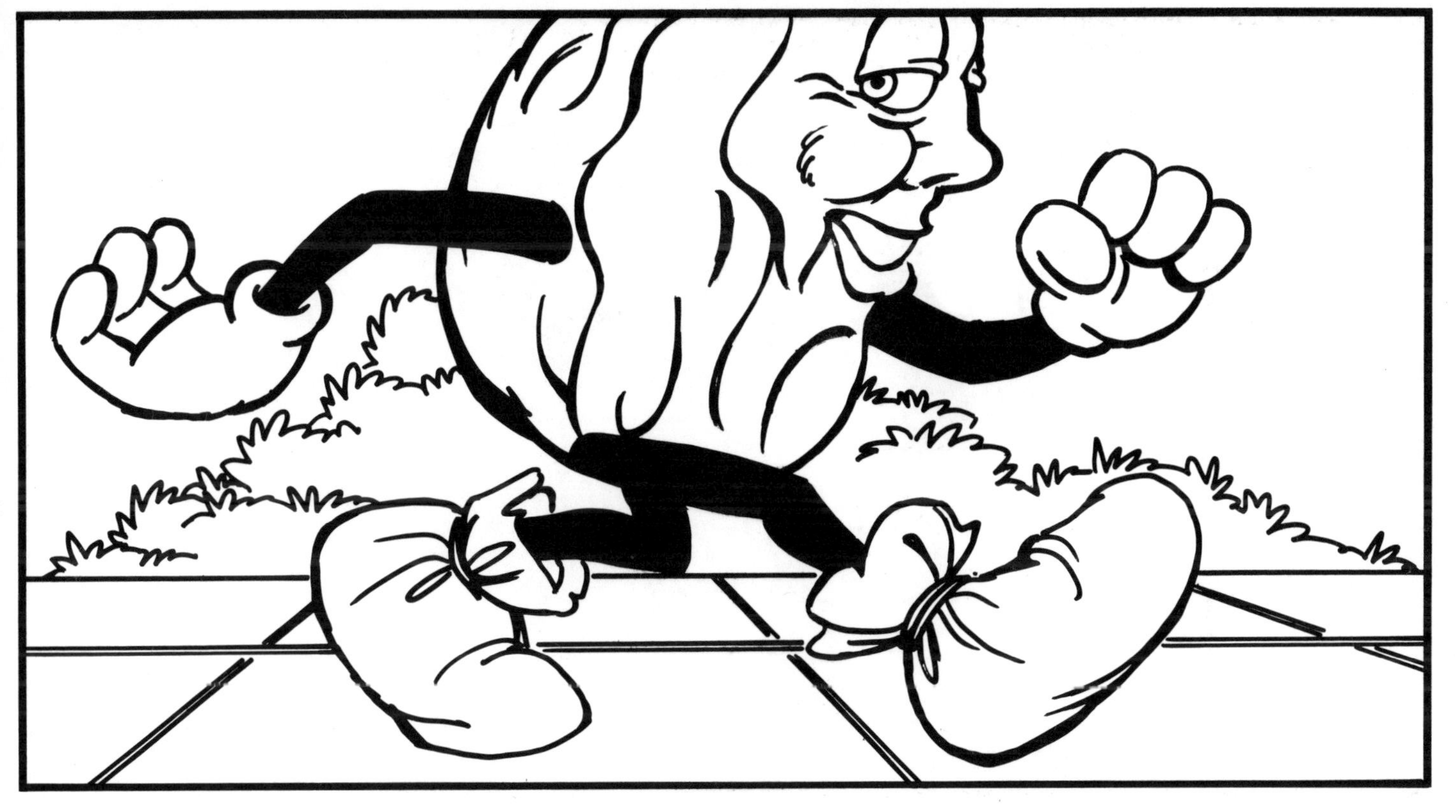

Wearing plastic bags over them when you go outside is not.

It's hot to drive to Las Vegas for the weekend.

Don't leave home without your wallet.

It's hot to take time off work to write that book in the secluded writer's cabin.

It's not hot when the "writer's cabin" isn't really everything the brochure said it would be.

Starting a band in your garage is hot.

Starting a band in your apartment is not.

Roller-skating to work is hot . . .

. . . unless your office is on the third floor of a walk-up.

Having a jacuzzi on your patio is hot.

Adding buckets of hot water to the kiddie pool on the back lawn is not.

Telling your friends you've got a luxury watercraft moored at Marina del Rey is hot.

Taking them to see your dinghy, the "Blazin' Raisin", is not.

It's hot to win a Grammy.

It's definitely not hot to trip up the stairs on the way to the dais . . .

Going to see the Dodgers in action and eating Dodger dogs is hot.

Standing in the restroom line and missing the only home run is not.

It's hot to take your friends to Huntington Gardens to show off how much you know about plants.

It's not hot when you mistake the poison ivy for the *Grandiosa floribunda*.

Cruising down the Pacific Coast Highway on a Saturday afternoon is hot.

Sitting in gridlock, because everyone else thinks cruising's hot, is not.

Flying your own plane is hot.

Having no place to land is not.

It's hot to dare to go on the world's largest roller coaster.

It's not hot to go on the roller coaster after your buddies have dared you to eat 53 bowls of Dutch chocolate frozen yogurt (with sprinkles & nuts).

Finding a house with "character and charm" is hot.

Discovering it's on an earthquake fault is not.

Going on a cruise to meet chicks is hot.

Having the same idea as 200 other guys is not.

It's hot to order in French in a French restaurant.

It's not hot when you have no idea what you're ordering.

Going on a movie studio tour is hot . . .

. . . Just as long as you can distinguish between what's real . . . and what's *not*.

It's hot to load up all your friends in the back of your pick-up and race off to the beach.

Watch those speed bumps in the parking lot!

It's hot to appear on the late show.

It's not hot to appear on the late, late, late show.

It's hot to have a gardener.

It's not hot when the gardener mistakes "blooming" for "pruning."

Shopping on Rodeo Drive is hot.

Asking the clerks for directions to the bargain basement is not.

Playing a big outdoor concert is hot.

Be sure the weather doesn't call for rain.

Barbecuing in your backyard is hot.

Forgetting about the burgers is not.

Putting a CD player in your car is hot.

Trying to wire in the rest of your stereo components in the car is not.

It's hot to be on a nighttime game show.

It's not so hot when the grand prize is a case of Auntie Hilda's Chicken and Giblet sausages.

Can you dig it? You should now feel confident enough to distinguish between even subtle variations of "hot" and "not." But if you still have doubts about whether or not to wear sneakers with your tuxedo, or choosing between luxury time-share condos in La Jolla and Pacoima, better cast those baby blues back over the preceding pages. "Hot" savvy comes more slowly to some.